PIES

Recipes, History & Snippets

For my mother,
a notable maker of pies

1 3 5 7 9 10 8 6 4 2

Published in 2008 by Ebury Press, an imprint of Ebury Publishing

A Random House Group Company

Text written by Jane Struthers © Ebury Press 2008

The Random House Group Limited Reg. No. 954009

Addresses for companies within the Random House Group can be found at
www.randomhouse.co.uk

A CIP catalogue record for this book is available from the British Library

The Random House Group Limited supports The Forest Stewardship Council (FSC),
the leading international forest certification organization. All our titles that are
printed on Greenpeace approved FSC certified paper carry the FSC logo. Our
paper procurement policy can be found at www.rbooks.co.uk/environment

To buy books by your favourite authors and register for offers visit
www.rbooks.co.uk

Printed and bound in Slovenia by MKT PRINT d.d.

ISBN 9780091930196

PIES

Recipes, History & Snippets

JANE STRUTHERS

EBURY
PRESS

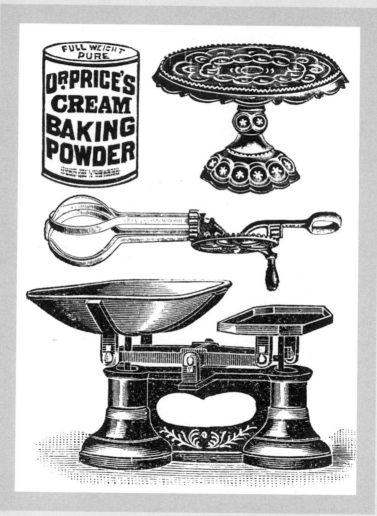

Contents

❧ CHAPTER ONE ❧

The Power of Pastry

He koude rooste and sethe and broille and frye,
Maken mortreux and wel bake a pye.

Geoffrey Chaucer, THE CANTERBURY TALES

Whether you're eating a sophisticated game pie or a simple apple pie, there is something wonderfully comforting and homely about biting into succulent, crisp pastry. Perhaps that's why humans have cherished pies for thousands of years and show no signs of stopping, despite the faddish diets that come and go.

A PIE BY ANY OTHER NAME

When is a pie not a pie? In Britain, a pie sometimes has a bottom but always has a pastry top. When it's topless, it's called a tart. However, in the United States, a pie is usually what the British call a tart.

The History of Pies

Pies date back thousands of years to the Ancient Egyptians who are thought to have been the first people to enjoy them. Their pies were rather different from those we know today in that they were made from oil, which makes for a rather floppy pastry suitable only for flat pies. The Ancient Greeks are said to have eaten a form of pie too, although details of these have long since been lost. And the Romans also ate pies, using two sorts of pastry. One, made from flour, oil and water, was only used to encase meat and poultry before baking, to seal in the juices, and the pastry itself was not eaten. The other, a richer style of pastry, was wrapped around small birds to be served at banquets, and was eaten.

When the Romans invaded Britain and other parts of Northern Europe, they took their cooking techniques with them, including those for making pastry. Over time, oil was gradually replaced with lard and butter, leading to the sort of pastry with which we're more familiar today.

Medieval pastry – known in Britain as huff paste – was eaten by servants only; their employers would discard it, its sole purpose being simply to create a solid container for the pie's ingredients. The flour itself was stronger than before, often made from coarsely ground rye, and suet was mixed with hot water to create an early form of hot-water crust pastry. Considering that clean water was something of a luxury and therefore people's hands were often dirty, perhaps it is just as well that most pastry cases were thrown away!

Huff paste could be moulded into a variety of tart shapes, called 'coffyns' or 'coffers'. One benefit of these early pies was that they preserved their meat contents for up to three months (if sealed with clarified butter) and protected them from contamination. Large preserved pies were often made by country dwellers and sent as gifts to their friends in towns.

Pastry gradually grew more tempting during the seventeenth century as the ingredients became more refined and sophisticated, with small sweet tarts made from egg custard and fruit being particularly popular. They looked elaborate and the

9

ingredients were chosen for their vivid colours, in the fashion of the time. Tarts that combined sweet and savoury flavours were also in great demand.

HOW THE PIE GOT ITS NAME

 The name 'pie' is thought to be derived from 'magpie'; a magpie is an inveterate collector of different objects and early pies contained a mixture of ingredients. Pasties on the other hand were made from a single ingredient, whether sweet or savoury.

EATING HUMBLE PIE

Today, when we talk of 'eating humble pie' we refer to having to abase ourselves in some way. But between the sixteenth and eighteenth centuries, the phrase was used literally. Umble pie was made from umbles (also called 'numbles'), which are deer offal. What umbles lacked in delicacy, they made up for in economy. As a result, servants and other underlings were given umble pie, while venison was served to the lord of the manor and other members of the gentry.

EEL PIES

Another popular dish from the past was eel pie. Both plentiful and nutritious, with a high fat content, eels were often served this way. In fact, Twickenham Ait in the River Thames, which was rich in eels, became so famous for the pies served there that its name was eventually changed to Eel Pie Island.

EEL PIE ISLAND

Upon this ait a house of entertainment has been erected; and here the river steamers are accustomed to land great numbers of holiday folks, desirous of the delights of pure air, and solicitous to banquet upon eel-pies, for which the tavern is famed.

John Fisher Murray, 1853

MAIDS OF HONOUR

The small, individual curd tartlets known as Maids of Honour are the geographical cousins of eel pies, as they are thought to have originated in nearby Richmond and Kew in Tudor times. There are various theories about how the tarts were given their name, one being that they were named after Elizabeth I's ladies-in-waiting at Richmond Palace.

He did give us the meanest dinner (of beef, shoulder and umbles of venison ...) that I ever did see, to the basest degree.

Samuel Pepys, 13 September 1665

11

Maids of Honour

Serves 12

600 ML/1 PINT WHOLE MILK
15 ML/1 TBSP RENNET
225 G/8 OZ PUFF PASTRY
1 EGG, BEATEN
10 G/½ OZ BUTTER, MELTED
50 G/2 OZ CASTER SUGAR

This recipe is made over 2 days.

- On the first day, make the junket by heating the milk in a saucepan until just warm. Take off the heat and stir in the rennet. Allow to set for 2 hours, then tip the junket into a muslin bag and leave to drain overnight.

- On the second day, place the curds in the fridge for several hours, until very firm. Preheat the oven to 200°C/400°F/Gas Mark 6, then roll out the puff pastry and use to line 12 large, greased bun tins. Prick the pastry with a fork. Turn the curds into a bowl and mix in the egg, butter and sugar. Spoon the mixture into the pastry cases and bake for 30 minutes until risen and just set.

CHAPTER TWO

The Fine Art of Pastry

TO MAKE SHORT PAEST FOR TARTE

Take fyne floure and a cursey of fayre water and a dysche of
swete butter and a lyttel saffron, and the yolckes of two egges
and make it thynne and as tender as ye maye.

A PROPER NEWE BOOK OF COKERYE, SIXTEENTH CENTURY

Part of the pleasure of eating a pie lies in the pastry. For the perfect pie, you need the perfect pastry. It should be a suitable foil for the flavours it will enclose, and it should also be made from the best ingredients. Cutting corners by choosing cheap flour and fat will betray you in the taste and often also in the texture.

Making Perfect Pastry

There are some golden rules when making most forms of pastry.

* First, your pastry must be kept as cool as possible (although hot-water crust pastry needs different treatment, as described in chapter seven). So, the fat you use needs to come straight from the fridge, the water should contain some melting ice cubes and your hands must be cool, too.

* The second rule is to handle the pastry as little as possible so that you avoid overworking the gluten in the flour and making the dough heavy. You are not kneading bread!

* Lastly, never stretch the pastry to fit the pie because it will shrink back during cooking. Instead, if necessary, create the desired shape or size by joining together some pastry offcuts.

* Pastry does benefit if it rests before being rolled out. Ideally, you should wrap the ball of dough in greaseproof paper and leave it in the fridge or another cool place for at least 30 minutes.

FIRST TAKE YOUR …

Pastry calls for very simple ingredients. Ordinary shortcrust pastry is made with flour, fat, water and a pinch of salt. For a sweet pie, you can use the same recipe or make pâté sucrée, in which a little sugar is added to the pastry mix and a beaten egg substituted for the water.

Puff pastry, in which the cooked pastry separates into deliciously buttery, wafer-thin layers, can be made at home but it's a laborious process. Good-quality, ready-made puff pastry is so easy to get hold of these days that there is little point in making the stuff yourself.

Normally, pastry is made with plain white flour. Avoid self-raising because it will make the pastry rise. You can use wholemeal flour, or a mixture of equal parts white and wholemeal, but the result will be much heavier.

When it comes to choosing the fat, butter gives the best flavour. Alternatively, you can use a half–half mixture of lard and butter or lard and margarine. For vegetarians vegetable shortening is an option instead of lard.

LET IT ROLL

Once you've made the dough, and preferably left it to rest for a short while, it's time to roll it out. In an ideal world, you would

15

use a marble slab as your rolling surface, chosen for its ability to stay cool. However, you can also use a large chopping board. Always make sure that your surface is clean and does not smell of any other foods – garlic and onions in particular tend to linger.

Now, dust the surface with a little flour, then place the pastry dough on it. You can also dust the rolling pin if the dough is a little sticky. If you're making a pie with a top and bottom crust, cut the dough into two pieces (roughly a third and two-thirds of the whole, the larger piece being for the bottom crust).

Pat the dough into a rough semblance of its finished shape. Now begin to roll it out. The secret is to roll the pastry away from you only, not to move the rolling pin back and forth. When you want to roll the pastry in another direction, simply turn the slab or board.

Once the pastry is the required shape and size, transfer it to a greased pie dish by carefully draping it over the rolling pin and then laying it in the dish. At this stage it will probably overlap the edge. Now roll out the second piece of pastry, if using. Arrange your chosen pie filling in the dish, then dampen the pastry rim with a little water and lay the second piece of pastry over the filling to form a lid. Trim off the excess pastry around the dish, then pinch the two layers together with your thumb and forefinger. Cut a few slits in the lid with a sharp knife, to let the steam escape during cooking, and decorate the lid with pastry offcuts made into attractive shapes. Brush the pastry with a little milk or beaten egg. Your pie is now ready for baking.

Shortcrust Pastry

275 G / 10 OZ PLAIN FLOUR
PINCH OF SALT
150 G / 5 OZ CHILLED BUTTER,
CUT INTO DICE
ABOUT 55 ML / 2 FL OZ CHILLED WATER

- Sift the flour and salt into a bowl. Add the butter, lightly rubbing it into the flour, using your fingertips. When the mixture resembles breadcrumbs, sprinkle over a little water at a time, stirring the mixture with a knife until it starts to form a ball. It should be fairly dry and crumbly, but able to hold together. Cover the dough and let it rest for 30 minutes.

- Dust a cool, clean, flat surface with flour and roll out the pastry into the desired shape, as described on pp. 15–16.

- This recipe makes enough pastry for a 22-cm (9-in) flan dish, to cover a 1.2-litre (2-pint) pie dish or to make the top and bottom crust for an 18-cm (7-in) plate pie.

Pâté Sucrée

200 G / 7 OZ PLAIN FLOUR
PINCH OF SALT
100 G / 3½ OZ BUTTER, DICED
50 G / 2 OZ CASTER SUGAR
1 LARGE EGG, BEATEN

- Rub the butter into the sifted flour and salt as for shortcrust pastry on the previous page. Stir in the sugar. Add the beaten egg and incorporate into the mixture with a knife. You shouldn't need to add any water. Form the dough into a ball, wrap in greaseproof paper and chill in the fridge for at least 30 minutes before rolling it out.

- This recipe makes enough pastry for a 22-cm (9-in) flan dish or will make about 24 open tartlets.

ROLLING PINS

A rolling pin is an essential piece of equipment for the pastry cook. Today, they are normally made from wood but in the past they could be much more elaborate, as sailors would carve decorative patterns in them. Very often a sailor, about to be separated from his sweetheart, would give her a rolling pin as a parting gift, perhaps in the hope that she would think of him every time she used it. Sailors would also carve rolling pins while at sea, and inlay them with whalebone pegs in decorative patterns.

GLAZING OVER

Tradition states that the type of glaze you use for your pastry varies depending on whether it's savoury or sweet. For savoury pies it is usual to glaze with a beaten egg before baking, whereas milk is most commonly used for sweet ones.

PUFF PASTRY RECIPE

Of the best kind you shall take finest wheat flowre, after it hath been a little bak't in a pot in the oven, and blend it well with egges whites and yolkes all together, and after the paste is well kneaded, roule out part as thin as you please and spread cold butter on the same.

The English Hous-Wife **by Gervase Markham, 1660**

CHAPTER THREE

Portable Pies and Pasties

Simple Simon met a pieman going to the fair;
Said Simple Simon to the pieman, 'Let me taste your ware.'
Said the pieman to Simple Simon, 'Show me first your penny.'
Said Simple Simon to the pieman, 'Sir, I have not any!'

TRADITIONAL NURSERY RHYME

21

Pasties and pies were the perfect medieval street food. Usually they contained meat or fish, and rough pastry was wrapped around them before baking. The shapes of the pasties, which were small, varied according to the fashion of the time. In the late fifteenth century they looked like little hats, and later they were modelled in the shape of peapods (known at the time as 'peascods'). The coarse rye pastry of the early medieval period was virtually inedible, so people ate what it enclosed and then threw it away (doubtless tossing it on to the street, to be trodden into the stinking detritus of medieval life).

Selling food was big business in medieval times. Not every home had its own oven, so cookshops, with their wide variety of hot food, did a roaring trade, especially among poorer members of the community. They sold a great deal more than just pies and pasties, and not only cooked their own food but that of their customers as well. Of course, there was always the temptation to charge more than the going rate, and in 1350 a law was passed in London which made it illegal for a cook to take more than a penny for wrapping a customer's rabbit or chicken in pastry and baking it. There were also strict hygiene regulations about the age of the meat that was sold, but these were not always followed, and cookshops were often accused of reheating pies and using meat that was past its best. Flies were a major problem each summer, and the lack of fresh water can't have helped. (It was common practice to gut meat and fish and chuck the entrails into the nearest water supply.) The need for clean hands and utensils was not even considered.

Tossing for Pies

Market stalls, inns and taverns flourished along pilgrims' routes and near the shrines they visited, and hungry customers kept the piemen busy too, as evidenced by the nursery rhyme 'Simple Simon' which celebrates their trade.

Piemen were still selling their wares in early Victorian times, although by then they were fighting a losing battle against the thriving pieshops. If a pieman failed to sell all his pies he would try his luck in the nearest tavern, where tradition dictated that he called heads or tails and his customer would toss a penny for a pie. If the pieman won he kept the penny and the pie; if the customer won, the pie was free.

Traditional Pasties

Workers out in the fields from the thirteenth century onwards needed food that they could eat easily, and which wouldn't be spoilt by contamination from their dirty hands. Small pies with thick, disposable crusts were the perfect answer. In some parts of Britain, these pasties became a celebrated regional speciality.

Cornwall is still noted for its pointed, oval-shaped pasties, with thick seams of pastry acting as a handle. Cornish miners would hold their pasty by its seam, which would become grubby from their hands and be discarded at the end of their meal.

The traditional filling for a Cornish pasty is beef and root vegetables, but there are now many different variations.

KNOW YOUR OWN PASTY

Sometimes Cornish pasties would have a savoury filling at one end and a sweet one, such as jam or apple, at the other. These were big pasties and, at roughly 325 g (11 oz), it was difficult to eat them all in one go. So the owner's initials would often be cut into the pastry before baking so that each man could identify his own half-eaten pasty.

The strangely named Bedfordshire Clanger is a cousin of the Cornish pasty. Its pastry is made with suet rather than lard, and it is shaped into a tube. One half of the clanger has a savoury filling, while the other is sweet, and a central pastry division stops the flavours converging. Suet pastry goes hard when baked, so Bedfordshire Clangers were wrapped in muslin and boiled for several hours. If eaten at home, they were cut in half, the savoury end being served with vegetables and gravy before the sweet end was eaten with custard.

The Yorkshire Mint Pasty is another member of the family. Unlike its cousins, it is entirely sweet. The ingredients are reminiscent of those for Eccles cakes, but with the addition of fresh mint.

Yorkshire Mint Pasty

Makes 8–10 pasties

275 G / 10 OZ SHORTCRUST PASTRY (SEE P. 17)
40 G / 1½ OZ BUTTER
25 G / 1 OZ SOFT BROWN SUGAR
25 G / 1 OZ CURRANTS
25 G / 1 OZ RAISINS
25 G / 1 OZ MIXED PEEL
1 TBSP CHOPPED FRESH MINT
MILK FOR GLAZING
CASTER SUGAR

- Preheat the oven to 230°C/450°F/Gas Mark 8.

- Roll out the pastry and cut into 8–10 rounds. Melt the butter and soft brown sugar in a saucepan and stir in the fruit and peel. Add the mint and divide the mixture between the pastry rounds. Pinch the edges of each pasty together, then turn it over and roll lightly. Prick with a fork and leave to rest for 10 minutes. Brush each pasty with a little milk, then bake for about 15 minutes or until golden brown. Cool on a wire rack and sprinkle with caster sugar.

Cornish Pasty

Makes 6 pasties

450 G/1 LB SHORTCRUST PASTRY, MADE WITH LARD
AND 450 G (1 LB) FLOUR (SEE P. 17)
450 G/1 LB BEEF SKIRT OR LEAN STEWING STEAK,
TRIMMED AND CHOPPED
2 MEDIUM POTATOES, PEELED AND DICED
1 MEDIUM ONION, PEELED AND DICED
175 G/6 OZ SWEDE, PEELED AND DICED
1 TSP DRIED MIXED HERBS
SEASONING
25 G/1 OZ BUTTER
1 EGG, BEATEN

- Preheat the oven to 220°C/425°F/ Gas Mark 7.

- Mix the beef with the vegetables, herbs, salt and pepper. Roll out the pastry to 5 mm (¼ in) thick. Using a plate as a template (approximately 20 cm (8 in) in diameter), cut out six circles. Spoon the filling on to one half of each circle, and top each pile with a dab of butter. Brush the edges of the pastry circles with water, then fold over each circle to form a half-moon shape. Press the edges firmly together and crimp them using your thumb and forefinger to seal tightly. Place on a greased baking sheet and brush with the beaten egg.

- Bake in the preheated oven for 15 minutes, then reduce the heat to 160°C/325°F/Gas Mark 3 and bake for a further hour.

- Can be eaten hot or cold.

CHAPTER FOUR

A Star is Born

Master Simon covered himself with glory by the stateliness
with which, as Ancient Christmas, he walked a minuet with the
peerless, though giggling, Dame Mince-Pie.

Washington Irving, THE CHRISTMAS DINNER

What would Christmas be without a mince pie – or three? Would Thanksgiving be as enjoyable without pumpkin pie? Some pies have become essential dishes, working their way into our psyche to such an extent that festive feasts would simply not be the same without them.

The Legend of the Mince Pie

 The buttery, sweet and spicy confection that we know today as the mince pie has a long and honourable history. Originally, in medieval times, its main ingredient was mincemeat, but this was very different to the stuff we use in our Christmas mince pies today because it was, literally, minced meat. And not just meat (usually beef) but offal, which was in plentiful supply and helped to make the more expensive beef go further.

By the sixteenth century, these pies had become a Christmas favourite and were called 'minced' or 'shred' pies. In the taste of the time, the meat was liberally mixed with dried fruit and spices.

A century later, however, the meat was no longer regarded as essential and was often supplemented by, or completely replaced by, suet. And by the nineteenth century, the meat had vanished from mince pies, although Mrs Beeton's *The Book of Household*

Management gave a recipe for mincemeat containing rump steak.

Medieval mince pies were small, but when the recipe was taken to America by early settlers they preferred to make larger pies that could be sliced up and served to several people.

HIDE YOUR PIES

The mince pie may seem innocent enough to us today, as nothing more than a temptation to be resisted by those with expanding waistlines. However, in seventeenth-century England it became the focus of legislation. Back then, mince pies were oblong, to commemorate the manger in which the Christ child was found by the Three Wise Men, and a pastry Jesus was normally placed on top of the pie. Such imagery was anathema to the Puritans who had overthrown Charles I during the English Civil War of the 1640s, and mince pies were duly banned for being Popish and idolatrous. They were only legalized once again by Charles II when he ascended the throne in 1660 (no wonder he was called the 'Merry Monarch').

The outlawing of mince pies hit the other side of the Atlantic in 1659, when many towns in New England (a strongly Puritan region) banned them too. There, they stayed off the menu until 1681.

Let Us Give Thanks

Celebrations for Thanksgiving, a form of harvest festival, have taken place in Canada and the USA for several hundred years. The first recorded Thanksgiving was in September 1565, in what is now Florida, although tradition has it that the first celebration occurred in Massachusetts in 1621.

Today, Thanksgiving is celebrated with a big feast to which family and friends are invited. A classic Thanksgiving meal features some of the foods that the American Indians are believed to have given the Pilgrim settlers when they first arrived in their new home. When it comes to dessert, pies are usually an important feature. Pumpkin pie is an essential part of a traditional Thanksgiving dinner, especially in New England. It can be made with either canned pumpkin or with a fresh one that has been slowly baked in the oven. Spices – especially cinnamon, ginger and nutmeg – are an important ingredient, and may be a throwback to old English recipes that used 'tartstuff', a thick purée of boiled and spiced fruit.

CHRISTMAS IS BANNED

There have been many religious disagreements throughout history, but these took a new turn in seventeenth-century England under the rule of

Oliver Cromwell. As head of the Protectorate (as his rulership of England was known) he exercised his Puritan principles to the limit through his Puritan Council. One of the casualties was Christmas. According to Cromwell, the festival was not mentioned in the Bible, making it nothing more than a wanton excuse for a pagan, drunken revel. So on 22 December 1657, just three days before the big event, Christmas was banned. Soldiers toured the streets, noses twitching for the telltale aroma of any Christmas food being cooked. Christmas church services were made illegal, too, and anyone who wanted to celebrate them had to do so in the utmost secrecy or face imprisonment.

CHRISTMAS AT DINGLEY DELL

Wardle stood with his back to the fire, surveying the whole scene, with the utmost satisfaction; and the fat boy took the opportunity of appropriating to his own use, and summarily devouring, a particularly fine mince-pie, that had been carefully put by, for somebody else.

Charles Dickens, *The Pickwick Papers*

LITTLE JACK HORNER

Little Jack Horner
Sat in a corner,
Eating his Christmas pie.
He put in his thumb
And pulled out a plum,
And said, 'What a good boy am I.'

Jack Horner really existed. He was the chief steward to the Abbot of Glastonbury who, during the dissolution of the monasteries in the 1530s, was worried about the fate of his abbey. Having decided that bribery was his only recourse, he sent John (Jack) Horner to give Henry VIII what appeared to be a large Christmas pie. However, instead of the usual filling, this pie contained the title deeds to 12 manors belonging to the monastery. Jack Horner discovered the secret contents en route to the king and allegedly helped himself to the deeds to the manor of Mells, where he lived after Glastonbury Abbey was demolished.

MINCE PIE TRADITIONS

According to tradition, if you want to ensure a lucky year ahead, you should eat one mince pie on each of the 12 days of Christmas. Another tradition is to make a wish as you bite into the first mince pie of the season.

Mincemeat

Makes 1.8 kg / 4 lbs of mincemeat

350 G / 12 OZ CURRANTS

350 G / 12 OZ RAISINS

350 G / 12 OZ SULTANAS

175 G / 6 OZ MIXED PEEL, CHOPPED

75 G / 3 OZ BLANCHED ALMONDS, CHOPPED

175 G / 6 OZ COOKING APPLES, PEELED AND GRATED

JUICE AND GRATED ZEST OF 1 UNWAXED LEMON

JUICE AND GRATED ZEST OF 1 UNWAXED ORANGE

175 ML / 6 FL OZ BRANDY OR MADEIRA

350 G / 12 OZ SOFT DARK BROWN SUGAR

110 G / 4 OZ SHREDDED SUET

1 TSP GRATED NUTMEG

1 TSP GROUND CINNAMON

This recipe should be made over a few days.

• Mix together the dried fruit and peel in a large bowl, then add
the grated lemon and orange zest, juices and the brandy or
Madeira. Stir well, then cover and leave overnight. The next day,
stir in the rest of the ingredients. Cover and leave for two
days, then put into sterilized jars with lids. Leave to mature
for at least two weeks before using.

Pumpkin Pie

Serves 6–8

275 G/10 OZ UNCOOKED PASTRY SHELL
450 G/1 LB PUMPKIN PURÉE
350 ML/12 FL OZ EVAPORATED MILK
2 EGGS, BEATEN
110 G/4 OZ LIGHT BROWN SUGAR
½ TSP SALT
½ TSP GROUND GINGER
½ TSP GRATED NUTMEG
1 TSP GROUND CINNAMON
¼ TSP GROUND CLOVES

- Preheat the oven to 200°C/ 400°F/Gas Mark 6.

- Tip the pumpkin purée into a large bowl and stir in the evaporated milk and eggs. In a separate bowl, mix the sugar with the salt and spices, then stir into the pumpkin mixture. Pour into the uncooked pastry shell and bake in the preheated oven for 10 minutes. Reduce the heat to 180°C/350°F/Gas Mark 4 and bake for a further 45 minutes or until set. Leave to cool on a metal rack before serving.

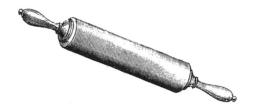

CHAPTER FIVE

Cheap and Cheerful

How good one feels when one is full – how satisfied with ourselves and with the world! People who have tried it tell me that a clear conscience makes you very happy and contented; but a full stomach does the business quite as well, and is cheaper, and more easily obtained.

Jerome K. Jerome, THREE MEN IN A BOAT

A pie can be a filling and delicious way to eke out a meagre store cupboard or to utilize the natural treasures of the outdoors, and over the centuries pies have often come to the rescue of the impoverished cook. But that does not diminish them in any way, as these can be some of the best-loved pies of all.

British regional classics that deserve to be better known include fidget pie from Huntingdon (see p. 45) and the Forfar bridie from Scotland (see p. 46). Indeed, J. M. Barrie mentioned bridies in his novel, *Sentimental Tommy*. Woolton pie, however, has achieved a notoriety that continues today, well over 50 years after its invention (although people who ate it at the time may believe it to be best forgotten, see p. 42).

The Bounty of the Hedgerows

Nature offers us many different foods, and lots of them grow in hedgerows. Would autumn be the same without blackberries? And even if you don't grow them yourself, a stroll down any country lane will provide you with enough fruit for several pies. Blackberries go deliciously well with apples, in a combination that's traditionally called 'bramble' (one of the many names for blackberries).

Stinging nettles may be painful when you brush against them, but they come into their own in the kitchen. They are rich in vitamins and trace minerals, and are most commonly used in nettle soup, although you could add small amounts when cooking spinach or chard. However, it is essential that you only pick the young top leaves of the plants, that you wear gloves while doing so and that you cook the leaves before eating them. Do not use the leaves of any nettles that have started to flower because they contain an intestinal irritant.

Perfect Partners

Some ingredients go together so well that they deserve their classic status. Chicken and mushrooms in a creamy, tarragon sauce make a wonderful pie, as do chicken, sweetcorn and onions, especially if you spice up this trio with thyme and a little fresh chilli. Faced with turkey leftovers at Christmas, you could put them in a pie with cranberries.

Steak and kidney is an all-time classic combination, but you could also use mushrooms instead of kidney if you dislike offal. Serve the pie with buttery mashed potato and revel in the ensuing compliments. Corned beef mixed with tomato purée in a double-crust pie is delicious when eaten cold with salad. And a hearty vegetarian pie of butter beans, onions, leeks and carrots, seasoned with lots of herbs, is guaranteed to keep out the winter cold. It's best made without its bottom crust, as are other pies using very starchy ingredients.

WOOLTON PIE

Most famous pies are remembered with fondness, but Woolton pie has achieved culinary notoriety. It was originally made at the Savoy Hotel in London in 1941, and named after Lord Woolton, then Minister for Food. The ingredients had to be flexible, given seasonal availability and the rationing shortages of the Second World War, but a classic Woolton pie consisted of diced potatoes, cauliflower and root vegetables, such as parsnips or turnips. These were boiled with porridge oats, chopped spring onions and a little vegetable extract, before the whole lot was poured into a pie dish and sprinkled with chopped parsley. The pie was topped with wholemeal pastry and dotted with grated cheese (if available). It was served hot with brown gravy, and was highly nutritious even if it failed to win any awards for excitement.

RABBIT PIE

In Beatrix Potter's *The Tale of Peter Rabbit*, Peter's father 'had an accident' – he ended up in a rabbit pie. As did many of his fellow rabbits because, up until the 1950s, rabbit was eaten much more frequently than chicken. Rabbit stew, casseroled rabbit and rabbit pie were all very popular. Rabbit was especially useful in times of hardship, such as during the Great Depression of the 1930s and the Second World War. However, rabbit became a less attractive proposition in the 1950s, thanks to the disease myxomatosis which was introduced to keep the rabbit population under control.

Today, rabbit pie is undergoing a revival, with many butchers selling jointed wild rabbit. A classic rabbit pie includes bacon, onions and plenty of fresh herbs, especially sage and parsley. Poor Peter!

Bramble Pie

Serves 6

350 G/12 OZ SHORTCRUST PASTRY, MADE WITH
350 G (12 OZ) PLAIN FLOUR (SEE P.17)
4 LARGE COOKING APPLES, PEELED, CORED AND SLICED
175 G/6 OZ BLACKBERRIES, WASHED
25 G/1 OZ UNREFINED GRANULATED SUGAR
½ TSP GROUND CINNAMON
A LITTLE MILK FOR GLAZING

- Preheat the oven to **200°C/400°F/Gas Mark 6.**

- Roll out two-thirds of the pastry and use to line a greased **22-cm (9-in)** pie dish. Arrange the fruit in layers in the pie dish, sprinkling over a little sugar and cinnamon as you work. Roll out the remaining pastry to make a lid for the pie. Using your thumb and forefinger, pinch the top and bottom edges together, brush the top with milk and make three small slits to allow steam to escape. Bake for **30** minutes or until golden brown.

Fidget Pie

Serves 6

225 G / 8 OZ SHORTCRUST PASTRY, MADE WITH
225 G (8 OZ) PLAIN FLOUR (SEE P.17)
225 G / 8 OZ BACK BACON OR HAM
2 LARGE ONIONS, CHOPPED
2 LARGE COOKING APPLES, PEELED, CORED
AND CHOPPED
1 TBSP FRESH CHOPPED PARSLEY
SEASONING
10 G / ½ OZ PLAIN FLOUR
150 ML / ¼ PINT DRY CIDER
1 EGG, BEATEN

- Preheat the oven to 190°C/375°F/Gas Mark 5.

- Roll out the pastry to fit the top of the pie dish, cutting a long strip for the rim. Arrange the bacon or ham, onions and apples in layers in the pie dish, sprinkling each layer with parsley and seasoning. Mix the flour with the cider and pour over the pie's contents. Grease the rim of the pie dish and fit the pastry strip around it. Dampen it, then place the pastry lid on top. Cut a cross in the middle of the pastry and fold back each quarter. Brush with beaten egg and bake for 45 minutes or until cooked.

Forfar Bridie

Serves 4

450 G / 1 LB SHORTCRUST PASTRY, MADE WITH
450 G (1 LB) PLAIN FLOUR
450 G / 1 LB LEAN STEAK, CHOPPED SMALL
1 MEDIUM ONION, DICED
1 TSP WORCESTERSHIRE SAUCE OR MUSHROOM
KETCHUP
½ TSP GRATED NUTMEG
SEASONING
1 EGG, BEATEN

- Preheat the oven to 200°C/400°F/Gas Mark 6.

- Roll out the pastry and, using a plate as a template, cut into four 15-cm (6-in) circles. Mix all the other ingredients in a bowl and divide between the four circles. Dampen the edges of the pastry and fold each piece over to make a semicircle. Place on a greased baking sheet and arrange each bridie in a horseshoe shape, then brush with the beaten egg. Bake in the preheated oven for 20 minutes, then reduce the heat to 180°C/350°F/Gas Mark 4 and cook for a further 35–45 minutes or until golden brown.

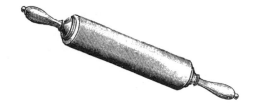

⇥ CHAPTER SIX ⇤

As Sweet as Pie

Good apple pies are a considerable part of our
domestic happiness.

Jane Austen

Few smells are more enticing than that of an apple pie, fresh from the oven. And it's just as good eaten cold, served with a big dollop of whipped double cream or some cold custard, or perhaps both. Sometimes, the simplest things are the best.

This chapter celebrates sweet pies in all their glory, and especially those made from fruit. You can make them all year round, whether you're using fresh fruit at the height of its season or bottled fruit in the depths of winter. Vary the recipes according to what's in season or in the store cupboard. Mix fruits together to make them go further and experiment with different ingredients and flavours.

A Countryside Flavour

You can also give classic fruit pies a fresh twist by adding delicious countryside ingredients. Try using sweet cicely, a herb that reduces the amount of sugar needed when cooking sharp fruits, such as gooseberries, rhubarb and blackcurrants. Candied angelica stalks serve the same purpose. Elderberries can be added to apples in a pie, and a spray of elderflowers (washed well to remove any resident insects) give a delicious flavour when added to a pan of fruit as it cooks. Taste the fruit regularly as it cooks and remove the elderflowers when their flavour is just strong enough, before it becomes too overpowering.

Apples in All Their Glory

Some pies crop up again and again. Take the apple pie, for instance. A traditional apple pie calls for nothing more than apples and a little sugar. Dessert apples hold together better when cooked than cooking apples, such as Bramley's Seedling (which turns to scented fluff if overcooked), and need less added sugar.

If you want to liven things up a little, you can squeeze a few drops of fresh lemon juice over the apples before you put on the pastry lid – this brings out the slightly lemony quality of Bramley's beautifully. Apples and spices go together perfectly, so consider adding a little cinnamon, mixed spice or a couple of cloves (but don't overdo it with these or their flavour will dominate).

Another delectable option is to add some dried fruit as well as spices to the apples, to make a Dutch apple pie. If you have some mincemeat left over from Christmas, you can spread it on the bottom of an unbaked pie crust, pile sliced raw apples on top of it, add a modest sprinkling of light brown sugar, and slap on the lid. And if there isn't enough pastry to make a lid you can just cut up the leftovers into long strips and make a simple lattice instead.

49

Apple pie does not have to be baked in a dish. Instead, you can roll out a rough circle of pastry and place it on a greased baking sheet, pile apple slices in the centre of it, sprinkle over some sugar and spices (if using), then gather up the sides of the pastry and pinch them together before baking. This method works equally well for other fruits (although a pie dish is preferable if you're using very juicy ingredients, such as blackcurrants or cherries).

The French have created their own version of apple pie, tarte Tatin. It is named after the hotel where it was accidentally invented in 1889 when one of the Tatin sisters let some apples cook for too long in butter and sugar, then fitted a pastry lid over the caramelized apples, still in the pan, and put the pan in the oven. The upside down pie was a huge success and a new classic was born.

Regional Delights

Another pie with several variations is a Bakewell tart (sometimes called Bakewell pudding). When it began life in fifteenth-century Bakewell, in Derbyshire, it had two forms. For Lent, it consisted of a spiced paste of ground almonds and sugar baked in a pastry case. But during the rest of the year, a sweet egg custard was poured over a base of chopped candied fruits. Today, a classic Bakewell tart has a pastry base covered with a layer of strawberry or raspberry jam and then topped with a rich custard of eggs, butter, sugar and ground almonds. A delicious alternative, albeit not a true Bakewell tart, is to use a good cherry jam as this brings out the full flavour of the almonds.

Manchester tart is similar enough to be sometimes confused with Bakewell. It too has a shortcrust pastry base, covered with a layer of jam, then an egg custard mixture, but it is topped with desiccated coconut.

Fast Food

When the soft fruit season is upon us, we need to make the most of it – fast. Soft fruits spoil quickly, and must be used when they're at their best. Benefit from seasonal gluts by baking the fruits in pies, whether in a single large one or in lots of delicate individual tartlets. Be inventive according to what's in season: raspberries and redcurrants; strawberries and rhubarb; peaches and raspberries; apples and quinces (grate these first); plums and greengages; or pears and blackberries.

Sometimes, areas that are renowned for growing a particular soft fruit have a traditional pie to go with it. In Britain, for example, Kent and Sussex are famous for their cherries, and the village of Ripe in East Sussex used to celebrate each cherry harvest with a pie feast – hence the traditional cherry tart known as Ripe tart.

Bakewell Tart

Serves 6

225 G /8 OZ SHORTCRUST PASTRY, MADE WITH 225 G
(8 OZ) PLAIN FLOUR

2 EGGS, BEATEN

2 EGG YOLKS

110 G /4 OZ BUTTER

110 G /4 OZ CASTER SUGAR

110 G /4 OZ GROUND ALMONDS

1/4 TSP ALMOND ESSENCE

GRATED ZEST OF 1/2 UNWAXED LEMON

3 TBSP RASPBERRY OR CHERRY JAM

- Roll out the pastry to fit a greased 22-cm (9-in) tart tin. Prick all over with a fork, cover and chill for 30 minutes.

- Preheat the oven to 200°C/400°F/Gas Mark 6. Place a sheet of greaseproof paper over the pastry case and fill with baking beans or rice. Bake for 15 minutes. (This is called 'baking blind'.) Remove the paper and beans and return the tart to the oven for a further five minutes. Reduce the oven temperature to 180°C/350°F/Gas Mark 4. Beat together the eggs, egg yolks, butter, sugar, ground almonds, almond essence and grated lemon zest. Spread the jam over the base of the tart, then pour in the batter and bake for 15–20 minutes or until golden brown. Leave to cool in the tin.

Ripe Tart

Serves 6

225 G / 8 OZ PÂTÉ SUCRÉE, MADE WITH 225 G (8 OZ)
PLAIN FLOUR (SEE P.18)
1 LB /450 G FRESH CHERRIES, STONED
2 EGGS
75 G /3 OZ GROUND ALMONDS
110 G /4 OZ ICING SUGAR
¼ TSP ALMOND ESSENCE

- Preheat the oven to 200°C/400°F/Gas Mark 6.

- Roll out the pâté sucrée to fit a greased 22-cm (9-in) tart tin. Cover the pastry with greaseproof paper and baking beans or rice, and bake for 10–15 minutes. Gently remove the beans and greaseproof paper.

- Reduce the oven temperature to 160°C/325°F/Gas Mark 3. Place the cherries in the tart tin, fitting them closely together. Beat together the eggs, ground almonds, icing sugar and almond essence, and spoon over the cherries. Bake for about 50 minutes, or until set and golden brown.

CHERRY PIE

Cherry Pie! Cherry Pie! Pie! I cry,
Kentish cherries you may buy.
If so be you ask me where
To put the fruit, I'll answer, 'There!'
In the dish your fruit must lie,
When you make your Cherry Pie.
Cherry Pie! Cherry Pie!

'Cherry Ripe', traditional song

CHAPTER SEVEN

The Upper Crust

Grouse pie with hare in the middle is fare
Which duly concocted with science and care
Doctor Kitchener says is beyond all compare.

Richard Barham, THE INGOLDSBY LEGENDS

Let's now take a look at the aristocrats of the pie world. Cooks have always been keen to create impressive culinary showpieces; some classic pies from the past were not meant to be eaten at all, but were intended to be stunning centrepieces that turned a banquet into a theatrical spectacle.

Culinary sensations

The pies themselves were intricately modelled from pastry, and often gilded, but that was only half the story. The fun really began when the pies were cut open. Birds flew out, rabbits leapt on to the table or tortoises looked around in sleepy surprise. It seems that the nursery rhyme, 'Sing a Song of Sixpence', isn't so far-fetched after all.

And there is more. In 1626, a seven-year-old dwarf called Jeffrey Hudson (described at the time as a 'rarity of nature' because of his remarkably tiny size) was concealed in a pie that was presented to Queen Henrietta Maria at a banquet given in her honour.

Ostentation continued to be a big theme at banquets and other special occasions. The Victorians were particularly fond of food that looked spectacular, with flavour coming much lower down in their list of priorities. It really was a case of feasting your eyes, but not necessarily your taste buds. The celebrated nineteenth-

century French chef, Antoine Carême, compared his highly ornamental patisserie work to architecture. In fact, some of his elaborate pastry creations were over one metre high.

Raising the Game

The Victorians and Edwardians were very fond of shooting parties at which country-house guests would assemble to shoot almost anything that moved. The sport made them ravenously hungry, so they were served delicious picnic lunches in which raised game pies often featured. These are made from hot-water crust pastry, which is moulded or 'raised' inside a special spring-form tin. When it's cooked, it forms a thick shell with a crisp exterior and soft interior.

Game pies are made from a variety of wild meats, but frequently from venison, rabbit, partridge, pheasant, grouse, woodcock or wild duck. The inside of the pastry case is densely packed with a mixture of boned meat, herbs and juniper berries, sometimes with pork sausage-meat balls as well. Then the pastry top is applied (leaving a couple of small holes in the lid) and the raised pie is baked. After the pie has cooled, a hot stock (made from the bones boiled with a few vegetables in water) is poured into the top through the holes in the lid and the pie is left to cool overnight. The stock then sets to create the classic jelly that makes raised pies so succulent.

If raised game pies are descendants of those fantastic medieval pies, pork pies are also younger members of the family, even if they are sometimes thought of as the poor relations. However, that hardly seems fair since a good-quality pork pie, or a proper veal and ham pie (with its central core of hard-boiled eggs), is delicious, especially when smeared with English mustard.

Pork pies are quintessentially British – even lending their name to a type of hat – and are exported all over the world. Recipes have often changed over the centuries: in the eighteenth century, Hannah Glasse (a noted cook of her day) gave a recipe for Cheshire pork pie which consisted of layers of pork and apple. A century later, a contemporary cookery book suggested using layers of pork and potato.

Gazing at the Stars

One of the most celebrated British pies uses oily fish, such as sardines or pilchards. The stargazey pie, as it is known, was invented by fishermen in Cornwall and Devon in the sixteenth century, where pilchards were plentiful. What makes it so notable is the way the fish are arranged with their heads poking out of the shortcrust pastry lid, apparently gazing up at the stars. Sometimes their tails also emerge from the lid, while their bodies, stuffed with herbs and onions, nestle cosily beneath it, resting on the pastry bottom.

Hot-water Crust Pastry

450 G/1 LB PLAIN FLOUR

1 TSP SALT

110 G/4 OZ LARD

225 ML/8 FL OZ HOT WATER

Sift the flour and salt into a bowl. Warm the lard and water in a small saucepan until the lard melts, then bring to the boil. Make a well in the flour and pour in the liquid. Immediately beat the mixture to form a fairly soft dough. Knead until the dough is smooth and glossy. Cover the bowl with a damp tea towel and leave to rest for 30 minutes; this makes the dough easier to work. Keep the dough warm by placing the bowl in a larger bowl containing a little hot water. Use to line a raised pie mould.

THE KING OF PORK PIES

There is the pork pie, and then there is the Melton Mowbray pork pie. This is named after the Leicestershire town in which it is made, and it is considered to be so special that it now has Protected Geographical Indication status, so that it can only be made in the town. The exact recipe is a secret but the pie's popularity has spread around the world.

SING A SONG OF SIXPENCE

Sing a song of sixpence,
A pocketful of rye.
Four and twenty blackbirds
Baked in a pie.
When the pie was opened
The birds began to sing.
Wasn't that a dainty dish
To set before a king?

TRADITIONAL NURSERY RHYME

A NINETEENTH-CENTURY GAME PIE

Cut thin slices of venison, sprinkle with black pepper and lay in a deep dish. Joint two pigeons, and a brace of grouse, and pack around the sides; take the best parts of a hare, two mutton kidneys, a teacupful of chopped mushrooms, two hard-boiled eggs quartered, and fill the spaces with diced bacon. A few forcemeat balls may be added near the top. Make a good gravy with the bones of the hare, the trimmings of the birds and meat, and a glass of port wine; fill the pie dish and cover closely before baking. Just before it is done, cover with a rich short pastry. Serve hot or cold.

Recipe from 1893

ACKNOWLEDGEMENTS

Many thanks to everyone at Ebury who worked on this book, and also to Chelsey Fox, Charlotte Howard and Bill Martin for their behind-the-scenes help.

FURTHER READING

Davidson, Alan, THE OXFORD COMPANION TO FOOD, 2nd edition (OUP, 2006).

Day-Lewis, Tamasin, TARTS WITH TOPS ON (Weidenfeld & Nicolson, 2003).

Fitzgibbon, Theodora, A TASTE OF SCOTLAND (Pan, 1970).

Grigson, Jane, ENGLISH FOOD (Penguin Books, 1977).

Hartley, Dorothy, FOOD IN ENGLAND (Little, Brown, 1996).

Spencer, Colin, BRITISH FOOD (Grub Street, 2002).